Fiona Wright | Knuckled

New Poetry

GIRAMONDO POETS

Fiona Wright | Knuckled

First Published 2011
from the Writing & Society Research Group
at the University of Western Sydney
by the Giramondo Publishing Company
PO Box 557 Willoughby NSW 2068 Australia
www.giramondopublishing.com

Designed by Harry Williamson
Typeset by Andrew Davies
In 10/17 pt Baskerville

Printed and bound by Pegasus Media & Logistics
Distributed in Australia by NewSouth Books

National Library of Australia
Cataloguing-in-Publication data:

Wright, Fiona 1983–

Knuckled / Fiona Wright

9781920882754 (pbk.)

A821.3

9 9 7 6 5 4 3 2

Acknowledgements

Some of these poems have appeared in the *Age, Australian Literary Review, Asia Literary Review*, *Antipodes* (USA), *Best Australian Poetry 2008, 2009* and *2010* (Black Inc), *Cordite, Cutwater, Going Down Swinging, HEAT, Mascara, Voiceworks, Westerly, Westside, The Salon Anthology* and *Softblow*.

The sequence *Inheriting Colombo* was developed under the Island of Residencies program at the Tasmanian Writers' Centre, with the support of the Australia Council, and Hobart City Council. Other poems were developed as part of the Western Sydney Writing Project, supported by BYDS and the University of Western Sydney; and with the assistance of an Emerging Writers Grant from the Australia Council.

Heartfelt thanks to Ivor Indyk and Evelyn Juers for their encouragement and support. Thanks also to Greg McLaren and Johanna Featherstone, to Adam Aitken, Jane Gibian, Liz Allen, Adrian Wiggins, Niobe Syme, Mark Mahemoff, Mohammed Ahmed, Peter Polites, Luke Carman, Rebecca Landon, Felicity Castagna and Lachlan Brown for their insight and friendship, and my colleagues at the Writing & Society Research Group at the University of Western Sydney.

For Claire and Alan

This project has been assisted by the Commonwealth Government through the Australia Council, its arts funding and advisory body.

Contents

The Waters

West

Inner West

The things you notice once you leave.
That here, the postman comes on foot,
the curled hairs on his bolstered calves
glowing ginger in the sunlight, his tourist-sized
backpack and boots. That here,
the garbage trucks are crewed and frantic
through the fiendish one-way streets and terraced corners,
and the bins are only buckets.
That the front gardens sprout bikes, or chubby succulents
but never grass, and you can hear
your neighbours singing, closing doors
and climbing stairs, can smell their evening curries,
and find their cats inside your window.
That here there are no teenagers, but Sports Utility strollers,
and even the retirees are tightly muscled.
That you can rent a parking space for fifty bucks per week.
The hairdressers are organic
and the dentists holistic, and the graffiti
is commissioned by the council.

Georges River

All morning we watch the river,
the mushroom smell of mangroves
        growing stickier with the sun.
The heads of divers break the surface,

just as we've forgotten,
their lips are fat and blue,
        and rubbery as rivercod.
The thin arms of trees scratch shadows on the water.

Police stand in scaly clusters,
arms folded over chests, the muscles of their mouths
        work in tight ripples.
Their voices brisk and stiffer
when they turn to us, and our machines.

Thick chains chafe the riverbed,
and the engine's thrumming furrows through the wetland.
No birds, it feels directed,
        there are suddenly no birds
and our chatter is swept up, and darkening.

The broken cars piled up
        like so many dead fish
thick and useless on the shore.

All morning we watch
the twisted bodies, dripping and slimy
from the dark water,
rebirthed, a cameraman jokes, a bit too loud.

Scratch

The acoustics of darkness, night clenches.
Feral engines. My heels'
ring is fragile and thin.
Each button pressed into my breastbone,
I curl into my coat.
The concrete as flaky
as winter skin, the shopfront shutters
scabby and reverberant.
The neon fizz from their glottal facades.
Kebab shops stutter and the sports club sings
in cascades; my tinny footfall.

I can hear each neckbone shift,
each beardhair scratch
the lulling voices   night,
as squared fingers
grit on shrunken coffee cups, and taut shadows
recline backwards from their hips.
The night butts cold against my car
and my hands bumble useless on the handle.

Key scratch. The thick silence of the engine,
the leather seat shrinks
its stiff skin against my own.
I don't want to say I'm frightened.
I'm not like that.   Knuckles

beat against the windscreen.

A woman's face distorts in the curved glass:
Hey! They want to know if you need help,
but didn't want to scare you.

Mona St

for Sarah

You forget about it, sometimes.
The open cut of this place, how each day
        feels as sticky and measured as cough syrup.
A curly child dips from her mother's black sleeve
like a tea bag.
You forget the metallic tang
of vanilla deodorant and chalk dust, the open cut
        of adolescence.
        Outside the Sports Club
blue backpacks bob and murmur
and station wagons herringbone the one-way streets.
        You forget, sometimes,
writing hours of evening letters,
as if you could pin yourself against them.
The classroom doors swollen under the humidity of hormones.
Chewing brittle fingernails,
        skipped lunches.
The buses grunt towards a funeral parlour
        with NRL-themed coffins,
biodegradable and carbon-neutral.
You learn to forget, most times, the things
that jostle and bruise inside blue backpacks
        and are never unbattered again.

Cannula

They enunciate, and ask him the date.
They pour ammonia over sound here,
they've forced a cannula.

Her viyella dresses are unbreathing
and she speaks on.
The corridors are convoluted as capillaries.

They pour ammonia over sound.
He wears his stepson's dressing gown
and she speaks on:

Everyone is using their first name, I can't tell who's a doctor or a nurse.
The man in the next bed was Macadamian, but he died.
You should have heard the hoo-hah and the wailing going on.

They like to get them quickly in the ground.
Your sister should get a job here, they're really understaffed.
Even the cleaners are black.

He wears his stepson's dressing gown
and does the crossword to strengthen his brain.
The corridors are convoluted and unbreathing.

They've forced a cannula
and serve jelly as solid as arteries.

My sister doesn't

My sister doesn't shop at Bankstown any more
because the drivers are all crazy, or else they all
hold both a licence and a pension card.
My sister says that Indians' cars smell of ghee and curry,
that dashboard buddhas are a hazard,
and Taragos are Beirut Taxis.
It's not racist if you hate *everyone*.
Or everyone who's ever tried to kill you changing lanes.
We drive in Bankstown in my mum's old car, on those days
when we're the pork that's roasting
out of season. My sister says the car is purple.
An African in a Santa suit
flaps a bell beside the car park, and my sister wants
to buy fur seatbelt holders from Big W.
There are too many one-way streets
and we get stuck on the wrong side of the station,
where 40-kilo boxes of washing powder
line up on special on the footpath and pigeons pick
at rotting lychees in the gutter. My sister says
she might buy a rice cooker for Mum. The sun is sharp
in the windscreen. My sister says the Greek boys park
without opening their eyes, or slowing down.
She has twice punctured tyres on the kerb here.

We drove to Auburn

It certainly felt like a Food Safari, such a long way from Kirribilli.
I'd googled Moroccan grocers, there wasn't anything,
so I figured that Turkish would do. Auburn. We drove to Auburn.
I didn't know it's so *economically challenged*.
The shops had no window displays. No proper signs.
The coffee tasted bitter. But we bought orange-blossom water.
And pomegranate syrup. So much cheaper than over here.
Although we had to pay for petrol. It's a long way from Kirribilli.
They served our pastries on a plastic plate.
The waiter wouldn't tell me what they were. He just said *biscuit,*
and *sweet.* And I'm intolerant of tree nuts, anyway.
We spent sixty dollars on wholesale Turkish Delight.
I know it's not to theme,
but we can have it with our sticky later on.
I think my off-the-shoulder embarrassed them. It's a long way
from Kirribilli. There was a Torture Rehabilitation Clinic
right next to the delicatessen.

Something has happened to Katie

– it was an *accident.*
Surf shatters here on Saturdays. The players grasp
the glazed eyes of sheeny-dressed girls, who slip
from bar stools to flexed biceps,
their pretty giggles.
Other men know their faces
from the telecasts. Buy them drinks, glowing amber
as trophies. Their wives smile shards,
they glitter mutely, poised on the edges of chairs.
Beer spill dark and sticky. Hands wander
in the backseats of taxis.

There is blood
everywhere in the unit.
Full-length windows over the black water, it pounds
like a hangover head, and she watches it, dark-eyed
and silent. The bitter set of her bruised mouth,
her hands ceramic at her side. The sirens circle
like gulls, the chip-hungry journos,
they both hide their faces.
We told the police it was you
how do you feel about that?

Lithgow Panther a Premier Concern

Its shadow pulls across her blinds,
drawn against the fleshy hum of afternoon sun.
Her fading armchairs, the stiff canvas of a big top.
She sees it moving.

                    Dark and muscled, she sees it moving
and counts her cats. The smell of damp straw,
iron bars and facepaint. She hears
its horny claws clattering her driveway, its razed teeth
gnashing on her rooftop. She sees it moving

And still they don't believe.
The newsreaders chuckle like indulgent mothers
and her mailbox fills with formal letters
drafted by public service juniors, who never saw
the crying clowns, the brown bears in jester hats
          visiting Lithgow.

She knows it lingers there, elegaic
and dangerous as Wollemi pine.
                    She sees it moving.

Musical Three

Adored. How the sound
    of four hundred thirteen-year-old girls can tear through
    any faceless city.
She hears it buckle
    her steel-shuttered windows
    her satellite security
some nights.
Its pre-pubescent fervour.

Adored. They taught her to be beautiful,
    and not to know it. Her hair is garlanded,
her judicious neckline,
dark eyes and a flashbulb smile.
Just enough internet interest
    for their fathers.

Adored. She wants to meet Bindi Irwin, she says.
The box office trembles.

And these are the happiest days of our lives.

Itsy Bitsy Yellow Bikini Helps Stunner Shine

Ms Dunne, 19, works in sales and said
it's definitely something I am interested in
She will contest the Miss Hawaiian Tropics finals
with a killer racing routine
it's thrilling.
Erin Dunne (pictured) encouraged
Territory girls to get involved –
competitors will dazzle the crowd.
you are getting up there half-naked in front of everyone.
The winner will represent us
on the Gold Coast
I just want to have fun.

Court told

The space beside her shrinking body
        as she sleeps. Eyelids thin
and pale as eggshells, laced collarbones.
Her cresting shoulders, softened arms
so heavily inert. Her dentures
and wedding band gleam on the dresser.

The crisp sheets will burn like newspaper,
he sees them curling, flaking to the ceiling,
floating on the hot draughts
of her breath. His own skin crackles.
        He holds the mallet, the matches,
a fuel can, the sheened metal cold
on his bare and veiny skin.

The smoke will hold them tighter,
choke the swellings in their bones,
their limbs will melt again, together
        like in the months that they first met.

I didn't want to see her suffer
the court was told.

Frequency

for Tara

A girl in coral and horn glasses
is discussing the relative frequency
of her massages and orgasms,
and how protein shakes
        are made from cattle hearts,
and how the sniffer dogs
might find the Valium in her handbag.

It's an Indian summer, and the fairy lights
asphyxiate a tree, the bistro buzzers
skitter on the tabletops
and she leans in close,
and chews her plastic straw
and lets her eyes grow wide
on the nervous man beside her.

She tells him
about a recent wedding, where both parties
looked like they were eight months pregnant
and how she's never understood
why lemons cost much less than limes
and that she's still black and blue
from horse-riding
and this pub really *changes* of a Friday
and she never should have listened to her mother.

Three women haul their prams onto the balcony
and shake bottles of formula
and order Bloody Marys.
A girl in horn-rimmed glasses and coral nails
grabs the man beside her by his nervous hand
and leads him out into the street.

Café Quartet

1

She looked bored until her burger came.
He spilt the water. She bit her lip.
She tied, untied
the scarf over her hair.
He danced his hand
towards the sugar dish
beside her elbow,
he picked a loose thread
off her shirt, but
she looked bored
until her burger came.

2

It's hard to look sexy
        on a beanbag.
He's swatting ants off the croissants,
        watches a big one
        winking up her ankle,
her sandal flaps from her toe.
There's pastry on his lap
        and she sucks butter
        off her fingers
before turning the newspaper's page,
transparent
        where she's touched.

3

He's pretending not to look.
His whole left side is stiff
        as if just thinking of her stroke
has left him damaged.
She wears lime-green frames and a cardigan
and he's watched far too much
librarian porn.
She swigs from his Dutch beer
and he runs his finger on its rim
and doesn't look.

4

She has stabbed the square of butter
onto her knife tip,
        and squeegees it across her fruit toast.
He holds the photos:
        a raisin-sized shadow
        swimming there.
She steals a spoonful
        of foam from his cup.

To The Children of Poets

To the children of poets,
on behalf of all poets,
I apologise.

I apologise for your obscure literary names
you'll spend a lifetime spelling out,
        or at the very least explaining,
        and helping people to pronounce.
I apologise for your vocabulary.
Your classmates won't find it endearing,
or quaint.

I apologise for the unwanted help
        you'll get on your English homework,
and for the years of books as birthday presents
when all you really want
is an X-Box,
        and how you might not have a TV
        or a microwave
        or be allowed to eat McDonalds.

I'm sorry for the evenings when you will have toast for dinner
        because your parents have been writing,
and the weeks where you'll eat nothing but black plums
        because they read about them somewhere
        and they sounded so delicious.

I apologise for the nights
        their friends will wake you
with bad puns and arguments over a colon,
        and for the blue cheese left to fester
        on the table overnight.
I apologise for boring launches
        (even if you manage to snatch free wine),
and for the strange skin conditions
        you'll pick up in second-hand book shops.

I'm sorry for the ugly boots
and textured jumpers
that will greet you at the school gates
        and for the endless cups of tea you'll be
so good at making.

To the children of poets,
I apologise
        for the imaginations you'll inherit,
        and hope you grow to be a dentist,
or a banker,
or a plumber
and will be able to afford good nursing homes.

Bruising

Eel Farm

For Jane

To her, they never slithered –
                    rather a rustling, the stiff
texture of their mystery
still dark and truffled
          on her tongue. They hung,

mummified limbs twisting
          from the smokehouse ceiling,
their mean eyes bulbous in surprise
                    as the walnut skin
          contracted from their sockets.

She kept the wood fire burning,
          felt the hiss and cracked static
                    across her face, her own flesh
          growing heavy on its flavour.

Test Cricket crackled
          by the dam, she'd watch her uncle sit
suspended like his fishing lines
between the brackish water
          and old newspapers: the hours of waiting
for the thin rustle
of their harvest.

Treehouse

It's dark now and we see
each other in the blurred glow of
other peoples' houselights, warm,
orange and so shadowsome,
the hollows of hipbones, the bare
luminescence of freckled skin.

I used to undress dolls here,
fingers
on buttons, zippers,
confounding as a bra clasp.

The whole tree
sighs with us,
larger now, more tangled.

The scrap timber floor
as brittle as the littered skins of insects,
or childhood daydreams;

unpractised, we move
like leaves.

Our limbs are awkward, intruding
        beside the tiny plastic chair, the tea set,
        the shorn heads of shiny Barbie dolls,
        their grins
                like the lecherous possum.

I think that lust, now
                will always smell of rodent shit
                and eucalypt,
and how desperately I need to buy a car.

Frangipani

The nervous tread of termites in the sill.
The minute balls of their jaws
spill, gnawing the warm wood
                        like handfuls of popcorn.
Between their tunnelings, walls whittle.

The ancient frangipani over-winters,
bald and bony,
            its thick polyps mottled and arthritic.
Its arms beg yogic for the sky, stream wider
than the shouldering terrace.
Cabled roots beneath the fences
            that hug the outhouse piping
            hollow the soil
            by hairs' breadths.

Weeks ago, barely, I bought a cardboard tray
                        of frangipani blooms,
from a wooden stall unfurled beneath my guesthouse window.
Their quick withering, the brown bruising
            leprous on the fringes of their skin
a barefoot offering
to the tooth of a god.

My bones grow cold under these high ceilings.
            The termites tunnel upwards,
drop their wood dust on my skin.

Liliums

The evenings have grown sharp now.
Light slinks through the slatted blinds,
        the gaps beneath lintels.
The scent of liliums on my opening door.
The shower drips.
A tidemark of baked soup
        scums an empty bowl.
Blunt male laughter. The crunch
of bottles through ice.
The windows fidget
        as the trains pass.
The scent of liliums.
Their split pollen pods
        husked on the floor.

Persimmon Poem

after Marjorie Barnard

At first cut
        it collapses like a slashed tire.
This translucent flesh
        a fecundity that defies politeness,
the tidy.

My sharp lap
        and angled fingers intrude.
Shaped like a young woman's breast, she said.
This fat and pulpy spill.

I am recovering, I too.
My mind as transparent and tender as new skin
in these,
        the blazing autumn afternoons
where light falls thick and desperate,

my vegetable garden glowing gold
        and pulpy-red.
I always thought this a female fruit,
                revelled in the lush tautology.

Seeds crack between my teeth.
The pit is pronged and angular.
I'm glad
        this portends a mild winter.

Kinglake

for Chewy and Ella

I

Short glass, the petrol gleam
        of the dark liquid. Expecting still
the black print of his fingers on its rim.

The terrible currency of searching –
his hands collect the downy weight of ash
and heavy emptiness

as others filled
with scattered teeth and jewellery.
Boiled flesh within water tanks.
White helmet. Monkey bars.

The smoke ghosting the rest of his platoon,
their limbs long and black. A silence
eucalypt and lunar.

2

How a burning piano must sing.
The years of oil on the cold keys
from your fingers' skin
mellowing the timbre.

The full-throated tenor of the flame,
the crackling wood, the sharpened ping
        of each string's tight, tuned snap.

Exploding eucalypts will echo in your chest
        years later.

Your orchard eaten into black dust.
I send you irises,
        and try to write
some kind of greening.

Inheriting Colombo

for Arthur

Harbour

They were mid-ocean when Singapore fell.
How narrowly they avoided narrowing
under the press of railway sleepers and wormy rice
        in someone else's jungle.

A surplus army.
The vibration of the ship's engine,
the vibrato of the birds,
the air hangs heavy with diesel fume and rainstorm,
        a shifting delirium of calls.

Trincomalee, the word dances
        the industry of dockers,
the curled syllables
        tight as bird bones.

My grandfather's tongue
limbered, loosened
        long before his body;
I have only these stories of his war.

Ekka, dekka, thunna, he learnt
one, two, three,
and *lassanai kelle*
                pretty girl.

Night

The rough weft
        of a mosquito net blown
against the face,
        the press of crevasses, and bones.

The crevasses of language
        I step outside and slip between,
snagged on their sharp edges.

The stars span
        the coastline,
the pointillist fireflies,
        the dark matter breathing between them,
the salty hairs
                sweat upon my skin.

A chilli seed burns
                and lingers.
Grains of sand in my shoes.

On a tincan bus, my thighs rattle,
                skin and vinyl
        in minute conversation.

The cradled oil lamps of a temple
          burr in the dusty window,
black ash curled on the hot air warp
                    and on my tongue:

raw, I am;
unripe.

Marching, Galle Road

All jungles are evil

LEONARD WOOLF

Bent palms can creak regular as metronomes.
My grandfather's thick boots pressed ridges in red soil
    as they marched south, spurred on
    by rapid-fire clacks of jungle fowl,
    the monkey's uncanny scream,
        the dark and viney rumours
        of other islands.

    The bored gazes of the villagers,
    the flapping of sarongs on tidy waistlines,
the ginger dogs with swollen stomachs.
    The soldiers slept under the thick weave
    of mosquito bites, and ticking stars.

South, they marched along the broken bastions
    of the fortress city
where skinny children
    dived into the sea, stole cigarettes,
where women sold them lacework. They would march
north again,
    limbs hardening.

Driving Galle Road

We ribbon between the rail line
        and the sea,
the city frays along its edges.
The driver sucks his teeth.
We both assume the other
        knows where we are headed.

Old men carve driftwood
        into curled awnings,
or bedheads coiled and knotted as their knucklebones.

A tin boat, bluely moored
        in a tree's branches.
Whole walls are missing, carved out
        from concrete homes.

A boy runs, waving, on a beachhead,
where fishermen pluck muscled legs
        like reedy birds
and lay their catch
                on wooden slabs.
The air tastes scaly and their skin
        is petrol-coloured, sweating
        flies like tiny gemstones.

We head south, ribboning.
The late rain prickles on my flesh,
and it grows dark so suddenly
        the headlights pick out lone stars
through the sharp lines of palms.
I don't know which shapes it is
        I'm trying to discern.

Fruit Stories

Banana.
Their Army wages were riper
        than all they'd known before.

This soft, misshapen weaponry –
bananas, broad and muscled cartridges
                on heavy stems,
spined pineapples,
thick-shelled mangosteen,
pomegranate, papaya, loaded with shot.

The round juice of new words
        on their tongues,
they sliced them thick in washing tubs,
and stole condensed milk to bind them.

In the suburbs,
        families ate rice,
                and curried Spam.

*

Coconut.
My housekeeper lived through one London winter,
worked double-shifts to stand nearer the industrial ovens,
won a street-side contest
        scraping over-priced coconuts with other ex-pats,

the white flesh
        fell away; flaked snow.

The barbed arm of her coconut-scraping chair
is uninvited and lecherous
        beside my leg.
My small hands on a hirsute shell,
the curve too globular and perfect
to hold unfumblingly:
        I will make a no-use wife.

That afternoon,
my pale flesh flakes
        under the buses' practised and hazarding gazes.

Cinnamon Gardens

Curtained by dark,
        black concrete and razor wire,
I see only the shape
        of the old army barracks, breathing
        where the rest of the city can not.

Streets away, a wall is torn
        in the empty imprint
of the newest bomb –

(the weapon curled against
        a pregnant woman's belly,

its budding nail shards,
the warm cord of connecting wire.)

In the dark, someone
        has painted the maw
into a mouth. Upturned. Screaming,
eyes pincered.
Thick fingers clutching the face,

and no one is willing to wash
        the image down.

Pettah

Packets of men's underwear thrust in my face,
the happy plastic
        of inflatable penguins, fat-cheeked dolls.
Spined fish dry on grey tarpaulins,
and piled red leather thongs
        grow stiff and stringy in the sun
        like the glutinous fried syrup
                children chew
                on long-haul buses.

The crannied streets
        stitch together stagnant roadblocks,
and tall and terraced houses
        lean backwards from the throng.
A sudden temple flexes.
Its sculpted walls
a mad and teeming mirroring of streets,
        the coloured gods bloody and riotous,
        vengeful as memory.

Fruit-sellers hang their washing, disembowelled,
        from razor wire
                and dice pineapple
                for hungry students.

I can smell war in this city, sour.
        The khaki jeeps creep through the bus queues.
A thin-fingered soldier
        invites me to hold his rifle,
and calls me beautiful.

Quill

Imagine spice markets,
        when his mother's pantry
        held only powdered pepper, salt.
Drinking avocado juice
        when the crocodile skin it was pressed from
        held no name.
The press of people, the buildings climbing each others' backs
        like football players,
        when he'd been born
        to quarter-acre dreams.

My grandfather bartered on a box
        built of porcupine quills and it was stolen
on his way home.
Those animals are now as unlikely as nostalgia.
He told me not to bring home a dark husband.

Colombo: Day Leave

Even the goitered cats
hypnotic and unmoving in these hours.

The suncrawl fractured
        on the lazy spin of copper pennies.
        Coins falling, thin and shiny.
The small puffs of dust
where they land in shrunken explosions.

Years later, we buy him scratchies for his birthdays.
Grandfather's always been a gambler.

The pennies fell his way, that day;
his debts paid off, they
        weighted every footstep.

The city crowded round – the fat bats
squawking over the dusty racecourse,
the *kassipu* brewers, the hawkers
                spitting betel
                tubercular, in gutters.

Years later, and he speaks like he can still
taste the fifteen dishes pulled
        from one mean chicken,

see the thick braid
        of the hotel owner's daughter
        sweep her shoulder, then the table
        as she lays the beer before him,

feel the thick beat of coins
        and red concrete
        on bare skin.

Arrack

The first time they drank arrack
they were found in a ditch
two days later.

The two man patrol
lying red and blistered, limp
as air raid victims.

The first place I drank arrack
screened World Cup cricket, and tracer fire
danced through the windows,

and gunfire smacked like red leather on willow
on final night. I was in Sydney
I couldn't know

the liminal shuddering of earth and sky.

Watching

My grandfather still talks
        about watching the city wells,
the water sheen like oilslick
on the loose, dark limbs
        of bathing women;
of teaching boys to shoot at coconuts.
He still talks of capturing a mascot monkey,
        its rapid syllabic scream
        like cartoon Japanese, he named it
Hirohito, and fed it from an Army-issue condom.

My grandfather still talks of trading teenagers
        three cigarettes
for fresh-caught fish bleeding from the gills.

How can I talk of the blue cotton dress
cowed by a streetgirl's lengthening shoulders,
        playing cricket
with an imagined bat and ball,
        as the ladies of Colombo tested perfume.

I ate white sandwiches and sushi
        at media launches
for stray dog charities. *(Paws for thought,*
says businesswoman). I swore uselessly

at the bandy-legged man
        who followed me home,
        his stumped tongue clicking.

I bought Sprite and spirits by the bottle
as white lights flashed and hashed machine smoke
flooded over lycra girls and robot-dancing men,
nursed an absurd and felted head
through the next day.

How can I write of the sinuous coil
        of trishaws around a mid-street shrine,
a concrete cobra's hood unfurled over the Buddha,
the threat of that venomous umbrella
precarious and beautiful.

I know my grandfather shot at the cobras
        susurrating into camp,
only holding sacred his own fear.

Earth

Motorcycles slow to match my tread;
there are no footpaths and my feet
grow dessicant
on the mild toxicity of insect spray,
the scuffed polish of road dust.

The liquid mornings bend
on battered buses, plucked chickens
        soften by the bus route.

My knees bruise
where I've been fondled
by hopeful commuters.

I bring their shadows home, marks yellowing
        in sickly gradients;
the dark dirt collapses
        down my shower drain,
embanking somewhere else
        as foreign soil.

The Waters

Old Jindabyne: Flood

The waters rose, cold as a chaste kiss,
and the cartography of our childhoods

we left behind.
Algae blooming where once
our fingers printed
the wrecks of banisters and doorhandles.
Old stories bloat and decay now,

and the currents tug
at church bells,
our cemetery ghosts grow gills,
barnacles and oysters cling like grieving widows
to their gravestones.

They say the clothes lines spin tidal
in our gardens of cabbageweed and grapeweed,
catfish, buried dog bones and buried pets.

They say that soggy shadows of ourselves
still walk on the old roads,
stand in queues in banks,
buy groceries in plastic bags, soft
and bulbous as jellyfish.

Now we skim stones,
          try to guess where they might land,
and fish in tin boats,
cast our lines toward the streetlamps.

Old Adaminaby: Drought

Silt, and minerals.
The brittling walls
now float on the waning water,

we see our old town excavate itself –

        and our younger wanderings,
                their corrosions and pockmarks
        grown obvious
        with the hard chemistry of time.

The cold water recedes again, and gloats.
The mud cracks into a hopscotch.
A fireplace,
        alone among the boulders,
        unmoored verandas like loose teeth,
        the boundary fences pared away.

The old roads are tightened,
        like our skins, and fissured;
We can see how much we've shrunk,
and worn away.
        Grown drier.

We touch the old bridge pylons
        with the silence and disconnect
of museums.

Walsh Bay

The old stilts creak,
        creak and clank
        in the water's plump lap,
lipped oysters cling to chafe-legged piers.

The new mirages
        of glass apartments,
slouch angular, metallic
        and insouciant as supermodels,
upswept on a hill's shoulder
        pinned between sky and sea,
        the girdled capillaries of lungs,
and the colander of bridgework.

This was a place where criminals
beat the sons of criminals
        with socks filled with wet sand.
They still taste it sometimes
        gritty and ferric
in seafood lunches.

Maggie: An Apology

We were emulsive-minded children
        on rickety and wrinkled knees,
and Maggie ghosts so darkly
        on the edge of our inheritance.

The vibrating shadows of
hazy days
        and hardwood;
The mute gazes of dairy cows.
An iron roof ticking in the night's tight grip,

blacking out the stars.
Its disapproving voice
        a ground-back constant.
Hazy days
        and deepslept nights,
        ringbarked hardwood.
Cowhides tanning wraith-like on the clothes line.
The consonant bird calls,
the thin newsprint
        that papered the walls.

Their heat-fraught,
        gin-and-tonic days.
        The high-collared women
        bickering more bitterly
                for their hardwood silence

the minuteness of their territory,
the crumbs of a housekeeping budget,
swept like saltbread fragments from a bar.

Cicada song
like a tuneless madness
ineffectual buzzing
and restlessness, and migraines.

That tethered energy
the silent tearing at each other

a frustrated daughter
running away along the rusty trainlines.

Thrumming through it all,
there's Maggie.
Her hazy gaze
hardening into cataracts and rheumatism,
and ghosting darkly
on the edge of my inheritance.

The Last Family Holiday

for Kim

Sitting big in a bar:
        curved and divisive as the equator,
finalities hang like clammy fairylights.

Plastic bamboo on the walls,
shirts budding and shameless
as cocktail umbrellas, and
no one mentions
        that the table is for three.
Our father

sips thickly
        from a coconut shell.
His nose peeling like a pink prawn,
his sweaty armpits and clumsy hands.

The barman brings pink sugar and innuendo
        to the torn coaster of my sister,
our father's grin
        is a tortured thing.
Our father,

still disbelieves
        the adultness of his daughters,

coughs at the uncomfortable evidence
of bad language, breasts and contraceptive pills.

His damp hairline receding to a widow's peak.
Tonight,
        he tongues around his cheeks,

grappling for the shape of things to say,
                (slow static of electric ceiling fans)
        'I've met this woman, girls.'

Morning: Ho Chi Minh City

Motorbikes dart like a school of startled fish,
fart petrol fumes, flick through
the strange melody of car horns,
their crisp and tonal language
        beating back the peddlers on the street
who hang from bamboo baskets
of fisty mangosteen and limes,
ricepaper rolls, tubular as a dissection.
The toothy men slurp soup
        on their haunches.
The kaleidoscope of motorbike mirrors
        silvers the boulevard and I don't dare
duck past.
Young men turn callisthenic in the park,
        smile as they kick their hackysack towards me.
The older women
sweep between the ordered piles of leaves.
The days roll slow. I buy postcards
of silk-tuniced women, printed
Vietnamese Charm
        and old propaganda posters
priced in American dollars.
Squid dry on cricked clotheslines,
the telegraph wires are kinked
        and knotted as noodles.

The evening breathes through the balconies
        where ex-pats share their chilli crab
and chilled cab sav
and tell me stories
        of just how they wound up here.
I taste the sting of possibilities, their afterburn.

Crossing

First, the dust cross-pollinates.
Guards in saggy khaki scratch
their noses, spit phlegm
before their stamps rubber
        onto our watermarked papers.
The road is thick. Wads of paper money.
Laundry bags,
and swift exchanges,
the litter of planky rickshaws
        and the speeding limbs of cobble-chested boys.
They drag past crates of cigarettes, munitions
        and pickled pythons, their bulb-like elders
sweep their hands and beam broadly at pink casinos.
Ribby women swagger under gemstones
        and rub their tongues over their teeth:
Perhaps there is no law
but human enterprise, the thick illicit
        and a price for everything.

Directory

In the late afternoon, or clear of morning
the highway bends and a factory flames the windscreen.
The rows of custom wheels spin,
where the sun's careen
torches the display window and shards off the metal rims.
Next door, the Salvo's warehouse peels
and lumpy plastic bags spill from its bins.

On a curve the expressway is wetsuit-black,
        it hurls white lines at office windows;
the layered buildings suddenly swell and stack
into perspective; backlit, scaly and alone
The thin tracks
of venetian blinds flow.
The gaping distance to the tarmac.

The first hairpin I ever curved without killing a silent cop.
It climbs a hill, then coasts the slope
right to the rolltop garage, a gradual stop
at the family home. The sky is pink soap
at dusk. There's a dent in the top
where my sister, in roller-skates, rode
her best friend's skateboard, and couldn't stop.

The Enmore Theatre promenade
where finding a park
        is the only thing harder
        than not hitting a drunk,
and the Mortdale station hill that jars
the tyres, stuck between potholes and trucks,
or driving through someone's front yard.

The road that turns to river in any downpour,
        where thick leaves slap
onto the windscreen like raw
eggs, where the spray caps
curl from mudguards, and poor
schoolkids hold wet backpacks
overhead. Their shivering thrall.

The M5 exit, where the cicada scream
        is louder than the radio,
and where the contraflow has slowed
down to a carpark. The light is mean
and glints off their blank windows
but it's just black and brazen road
in front, and I'm alone.

Pacific Song

The cheeks of children
        squash against the windows
and the heads of dogs flap out,
their spittle sprinkles back beside the rain.
We cross the Hawkesbury, Holt-Bragg,
        Mooney-Mooney, Hunter,
and dream of breakwalls, and bindi-eyes,
the tarmac unrolling beneath us.
The bulldozers sleep in clay soil.
Women paint fingernails on the dashboard
and fiddle for radio reception.
Bike wheels pedal furiously
in the slipstream of towbars,
canoes and kayaks float on roof-racks,
and we worry the salted occy-straps
that snap them down.
Hibiscus print dizzies each weatherproof cover.
We pass Ridgey-Didge Pies
        and the Driver Reviver,
        and squabble over leg-spreads
and car-farts.
Two straw hats are decoyed
        on the back dash of a sedan.
We dream. We drive. It drizzles,
        and yet we dream of sandbars,
and redbrick amenities, of tents.

Of splashing our feet under taps.
We pull faces at waving children
crammed beside beach towels, beside sun shades,
beside laundry bags and eskies. The road is as familiar
as a pillowcase. Oh, how we dream, we dream
of chip shops and oysterbeds, of baitsheds and lobster-pots.
Of asbestos-creted unit blocks,
of temperamental coin-op barbecues, and pineapple rings
on their burnt tops and roads named Main St,
Beach St, Ocean Rd. We dream.
We dream, and hug the wet bitumen, pacific.

Ulladulla

Each year the road winds a little less,
the clustered coastal towns
        bypassed progressively:
to local traffic only,
to long twilights, saltburn
and white ants.

We know each car's trajectory now,
who'll stop just out of Nowra for strawberry milk and petrol,
who detours to the blowhole,
or delays their toilet stop
        until the crumbling doughnut shop
        on High Street.

What it is that makes tradition out of chance:
The kilo box of stonefruit
        that turns our stomachs hard and round
        as peach pips overnight,
the stubborn chaos of communal grocery shopping,
        the fridge filled with strings of sausages
        longer than all our intestines combined.

We stack the beer fridge, stand
        windswept on the headland,
feed our ankles to wet sand
as the first night waves hiss towards the dark,
                inexorable as breath, as earsong.

Rock Pool

for Thomasen

Some hardness there dissolves.
This place carved out of cliffstones.
        The porous rock planed
with the abrasion of insteps,

        the larger smoothness
                an accidental grace
that we forget
when the salt scent has dried from the air.

The purled water
        and the memory of their flesh,
their swimcaps, frilled as algae,
the vegetable buoyancy
        of loose and ageing skin.
It's a leonine tribe here now.

Their dappled bodies limpet-like on stone,
the glint off salt crystals
        that pelt on downy skin.
Muscular rustling as our footsteps
fall like trespass.
I crush periwinkles underneath my feet.

Handbags cradle in the rock, grow strange
and polyped as dead coral.
                    We abandon
our politeness, our prickly, anemone selves
to the salt kiss and puddle,
green our skin
beneath the water's stinging lip, we swim
lazy orbits.
The alchemy of salt and sunshine.
          A spongiform language
between us.

The Baigneur

When their skirts swell in the flouncing water
like the thick wave
of a stingray, and their hair
grows weedlike on their cheeks,
and their eyes
are as swift as shoaled fish,
that's when I know
          I'm needed most.

          Their limbs slacken,
then grow taut: there's a seabeast,
instinctual, in us all.

The water foams their thighs,
and they stumble when they stand,
their own weight foreign to their footing.
Sometimes their toes break through the surface
          in pink panic,
and they grip my hairy hand.

But we wear black, slick as performing seals
and we stare seaward, count the rhythm
of the breaking waves,
          we guide them into shore.

The children aren't as strenuous.
They're used to abandonment
and thrall.

West Coast

We play at metaphor.
A tingle tree is hollow, burnt out at its core,
but grows more robust for it.
A storm cloud shows so many shades of grey.
Insects suicide against the windscreen.

I'm reading Hewett, though, and know
that a peppermint tree
is a peppermint tree,
and brutally specific.

The horizon at day's limit is dusted road-red.
Sheets of light that seem solid enough to hold our weight
sweep rays like windy surfers in to shore.
It is stone that crumbles.

The saltbush is crusted vermilion.
My nose runs in the cold air
and you think I might be crying.
You hold your plastic teacup
        as if to catch the light inside its fat, white rim
and call me irrepressible.
I like that.

Honey

I'm wearing a little thin
        dress and the space
between buildings and sky honeys.
The road narrows – this,
the treacle time of day
        when dogs spill their tongues
        under fading hydrangeas
and there's a meltdown of population. How crisp
the lines of buildings, tethering
zebra crossings to broken phone booths,
the hilled horizon
        to the highway shuddering by.

Scarborough

We have buffeted our backs against the ocean.
Bouldered and eroded,
        we spread our beach towels on the grass.
This is salt. My chest is chambered.
We have outstood it,
the road. There's a gravity to hairpin bends.

Behind, a frizzy couple upend shandies
        and share a crossword.
Escarpment. The sharpness nestled in the very word.
Our plate of squid tenses,
        the suckered tentacles hollowed.
Cow-weed yellows on the train line. This salt,

dessicant and leaching.
The bowl of ocean sweeps us,
and we are good. We have
outstood.

Notes

Page Three Girls: Each poem takes its title, and some lines, from an article that appeared on page three of a newspaper, as follows:
'Despite Court Order, Bird's Agent Sees Girlfriend', *SMH,* 27/08/08. The italicised lines, quoted in the article, form a text message sent by NRL footballer Greg Bird to his housemate, after his arrest for assaulting his girlfriend Katie, with a broken glass.
'Lithgow Panther a Premier Concern,' *SMH*, 20/09/08
'Itsy Bitsy Yellow Bikini Helps Stunner Shine,' *The Territorian*, 23/11/08
'The Happiest Days of Our Lives', *SMH*, 11/11/08
'Husband wanted to end it all, Court told,' *SMH*, 12/09/08

Harbour: Trincomalee is a deep-water harbour on the west coast of Sri Lanka, used as a major naval base during the Second World War. It was also a heavily contested area in the war between the Sri Lankan government and Tamil Tigers.

Colombo: Day Leave: Kassipu is a kind of moonshine alcohol, now illegal.

Marching: Quote from Leonard Woolf, *A Village in the Jungle*, Hogarth Press, 1913.

Persimmon Poem: The italicised lines are from Marjorie Barnard's story 'The Persimmon Tree', *The Persimmon Tree and other stories*, Virago Press, 1985.

The Baigneur: At the turn of the last century, wealthy holiday-makers on the Crimean coast would hire a baigneur to assist them when they went swimming in the ocean, in case the waves became too fierce. They are an important presence in Vladimir Nabokov's *Speak Memory* (Penguin).